CITY SYMBOLS

Marcia Divona & Barbara Shaw

Art Direction Book Company - New York

Publisher:
Art Direction Book Company
10 East 39th Street
New York, NY 10016

ISBN 0-88108-115-9 cloth
ISBN 0-88108-116-7 paper
LCC# 93-701360

The information contained herein has been obtained from sources we deam
reliable. While we have no reason to doubt its accuracy, we do not guarantee it.
We regret and apologize for any errors or deletions in names, dates and population
figures or typographic errors.

ACKNOWLEDGEMENTS

This project took more time and patience to complete than we had anticipated. We wish to thank all city staffs for their submissions, without which this book would not be possible. Our deepest thanks goes out to Brian Benlifer for his suggestions and support and to Mark Moore for his advice.

TABLE OF CONTENTS

INTRODUCTION

City Symbols is a reference for designers, architects, city planners and municipal graphic departments. This book depicts a comprehensive selection of contemporary city logos and illustrates to the reader exactly what other cities have produced, inspires the creative process and eliminates duplication. It is an invaluable resource for any city staff that wants to update its image.

Municipalities are realizing now what people in the commercial sector have known for a long time, image helps to create awareness and perception. Today, few cities, large or small, can rely on a complacent population and a stable tax base to maintain and improve their services and facilities. Instead, they must compete for tourism, industry and grants in order to prosper.

Our aim is to showcase city logo design in this book; however, the seal is still used as an all-purpose symbol by many cities. Because we had to rely on submissions, this reference has a mixture of the traditional seal and the contemporary graphic symbol or logo.

In some cities the Chamber of Commerce, Tourist Bureau, Parks & Recreation Departments or other groups use graphic symbols for their ads or brochures and these symbols are subsequently adopted as official city logos.

Note: In the following order beside each logo you will find the name of the city, the population as of 1980 or later, the designer when provided and the year of the design when provided.

PASS WITH CARE

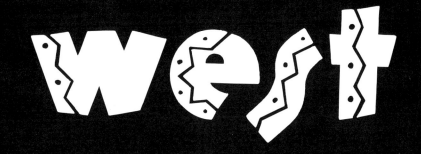

ALASKA

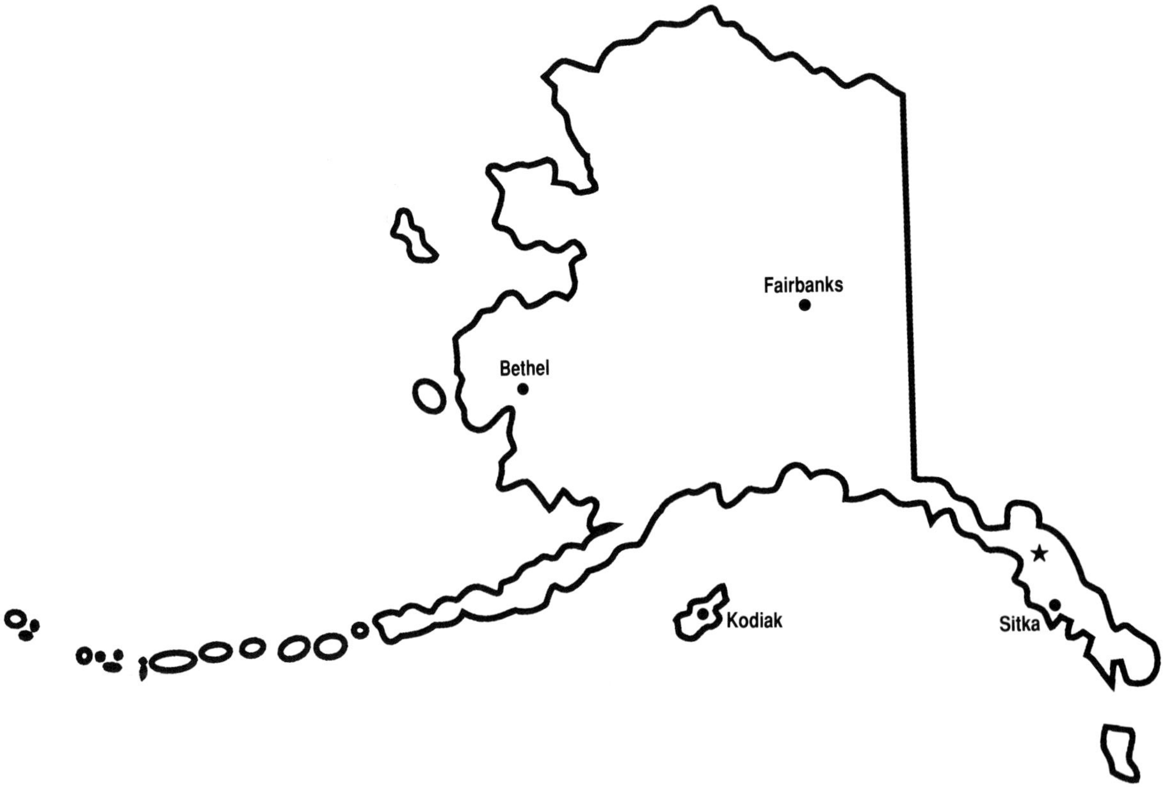

Fairbanks
•

Bethel
•

Kodiak
•

Sitka
•

Kodiak
6,774
1984

Sitka
8,500
1971

Bethel
4,504

Fairbanks
30,000

ARIZONA

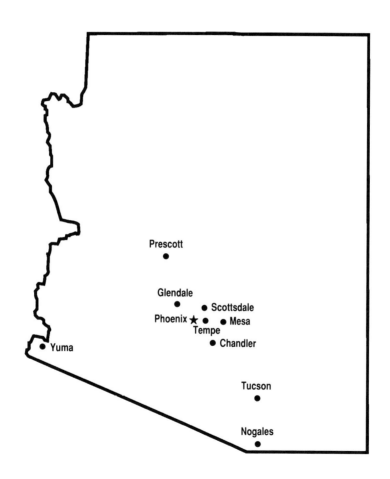

Mesa
301,000
city staff
1986

Phoenix
1,000,000
competition/Smit Ghormley Sanft
1987

CITY OF
NOGALES

Nogales
20,000
Louis Valenzuela
1990

Prescott
25,000
1952

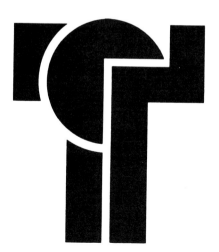

Tempe
145,548
competition/Joe Scuderi,
   student, Arizona State
   University

Tucson
409,490
competition/Mrs. Norman Crowfoot
1949

Scottsdale
111,140

Yuma
55,000
city staff
1980

AZ

Glendale
143,000
city staff
1989

Chandler
91,000
competition/Arizona State
  University Art Department

17

CALIFORNIA

Huntington Beach
190,000
competition/John Casado
1968

Napa
57,863
1987

Mt. Shasta
3,552
Nadine Aiello
1985

CITY OF MOUNTAIN VIEW

Mountain View
63,500
Michele Roberts
 City Logo 1981
 Downtown 1985
Jane Anderson
 Shoreline 1983

DOWNTOWN
MOUNTAIN VIEW

SHORELINE
AT·MOUNTAIN·VIEW

Long Beach
419,819
competition/Paul Showalter
1989

Santa Ana
237,300
city staff
1990

Anaheim
244,150
1987

Cotati
5,200
Randy L. Johnsen &
Linda Shearer Rook
1988

Eureka
24,803

COLORADO

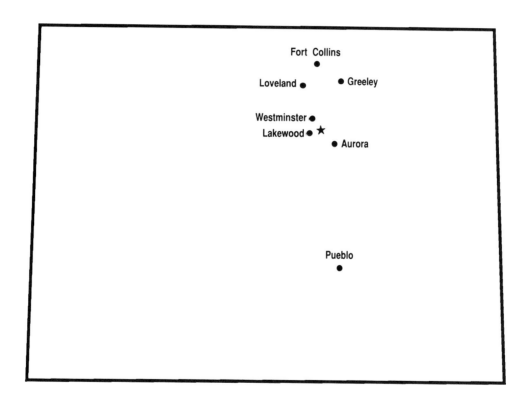

Fort Collins
●

Loveland ● ● Greeley

Westminster ●
Lakewood ● ★
● Aurora

Pueblo
●

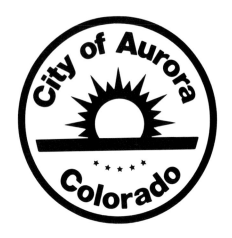

Aurora
230,000
Albert Christen
1950's
Parks & Recreation Dept.
Debbie Whitehouse Jones
1970
Kay Clymer
1989
Kay Clymer
1988

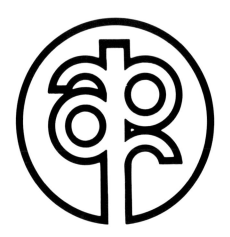

Ft. Collins
88,000
Kathleen Tracey
1988

Lakewood
125,000
1978

CO

"The logo symbol represents the most positive aspect of the City of Pueblo being the sun. It reflects the natural light and brightness of the area and is strong enough to stand on its own. The logo symbol's main function is to accent the word "PUEBLO" in special script by drawing attention to the name and reinforcing the public's positive attitude toward the City of Pueblo."

Pueblo
101,240
1978

Westminster
76,000
1988

Greeley
62,000
city staff
1980

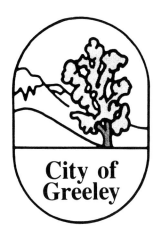

Loveland
38,000
Darrel Smith
1987

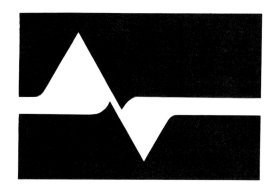

HAWAII

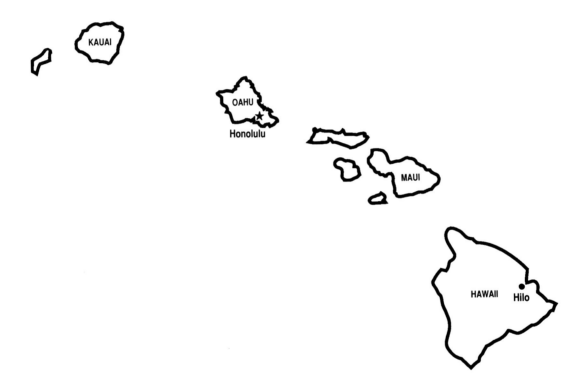

Honolulu
893,100
Viggo Jacobsen
1909

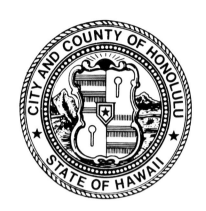

Hilo
117,500
1976

IDAHO

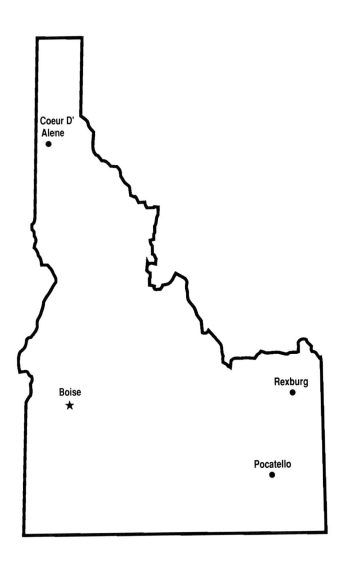

Coeur D'
Alene
●

Rexburg
●

Boise
★

Pocatello
●

Boise
130,000
Elgin Syferd Drake Inc.
  Ruth Fritz
1990

Coeur d'Alene
24,563
Hanna/Wheeler & Associates
1982

ID

Rexburg
12,084
competition/Ricks College
1982

Pocatello
45,334
1989

MONTANA

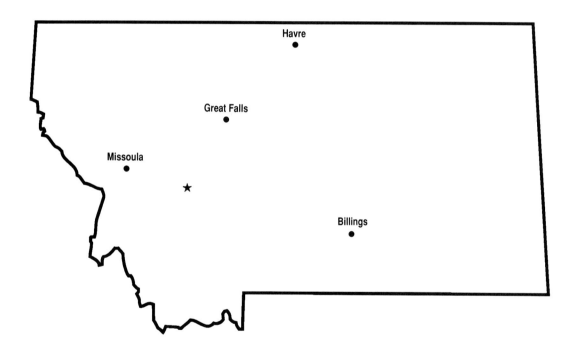

Havre
●

Great Falls
●

Missoula
●

★

Billings
●

MT

Billings
80,100
Fernando M. Mendez
1986

Great Falls
58,000
Advanced Litho Printing
1989

Havre
10,300

Missoula
33,388
city staff
1983

NEVADA

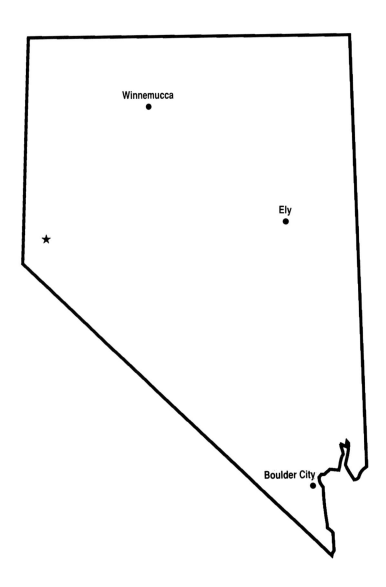

Winnemucca

Ely

Boulder City

Boulder City
13,500
city staff
1985

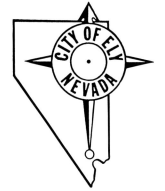

Ely
5,000
1970

Winnemucca
6,150

NEW MEXICO

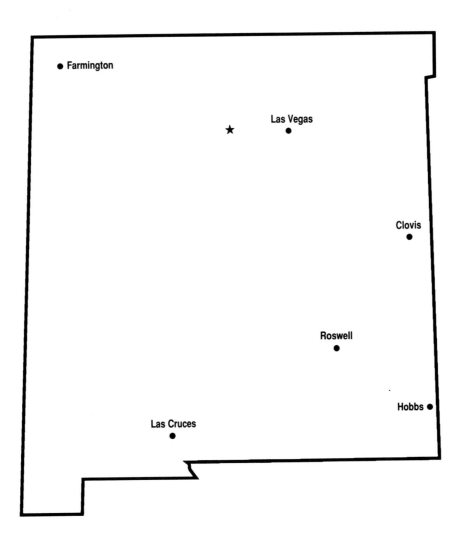

Farmington

Las Vegas

Clovis

Roswell

Hobbs

Las Cruces

Clovis
32,000
city staff
1989

Farmington
37,000
city staff
1972

Las Cruces
54,090

Roswell
46,000
William Brainerd
1986

Hobbs
25,000

Las Vegas
15,000
Patrick McDermott
1982

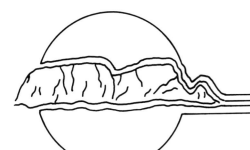

OREGON

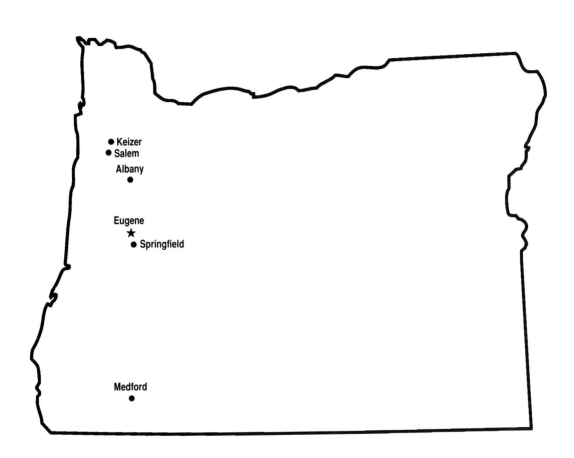

● Keizer
● Salem
Albany
●

Eugene
★
● Springfield

Medford
●

OR

Eugene
120,000
city staff
1979

Albany
29,375
Lynn Powers
1990

Medford
46,500
Parks & Recreation Dept.
Laura Kay
1989

designer unknown
1973

Keizer
20,585
competition
This logo is a combination of
two winning entries: the city's
motto "Pride, Spirit and Vol-
unteerism" is represented by
the three stars and the gradu-
ated lines represent growth
and the future; 1982 is the
year of incorporation.
1983

OR

Salem
107,786
competition/Waren Carkin
1972

Springfield
44,000
Betsy Ford, Graphics Unlimited
1986

TEXAS

Lubbock

Garland

Dallas ● Mesquite

Arlington ●

Odessa

● El Paso

★

Beaumont

Corpus Christi ●

McAllen

TX

Odessa
89,699
William R. Brown, Jr.
Vicki Watson
1990

Dallas
1,003,520

Lubbock
194,148
Jester Art Gallery

El Paso
491,800

...at the Corner of
Texas and Old Mexico.

Beaumont
117,000
Barbara Hansen
1971

Corpus Christi
274,476
1989

Arlington
249,770
city staff
1973

McAllen
90,000
Rodd & Associates Advertising
1988

Mesquite
103,550
Crawford Dunn
1966

Garland
184,000
Jess Green Advertising
1971

UTAH

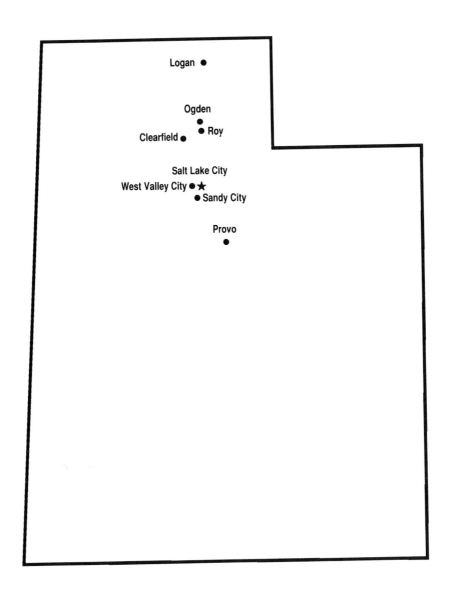

Logan ●

Ogden
●
● Roy

Clearfield ●

Salt Lake City
West Valley City ● ★
● Sandy City

Provo
●

Salt Lake City
153,000

PUBLIC WORKS

UT

Roy
28,000
Rainbow Graphics
1990

Sandy City
80,000

Logan
35,000
city staff
1976

Ogden
65,000

Development Services
Rick Jones
1989

Provo
84,000
Hales Allen Company
1989

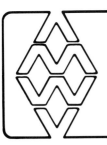 West Valley City

West Valley City
100,000
city staff
1983

Clearfield City

proud of our past .... keeping pace with the future

Clearfield
24,000
Jeff Hepworth
1986

WASHINGTON

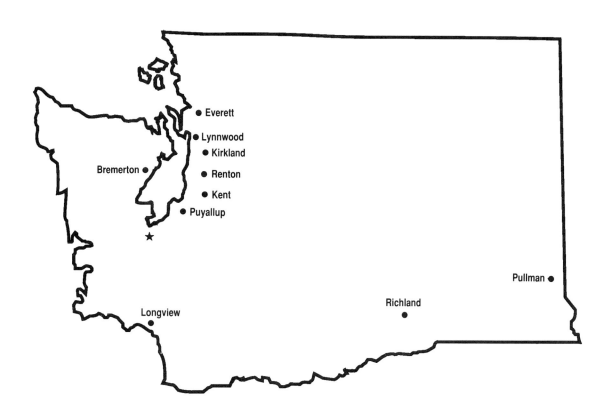

Everett

Lynnwood

Kirkland

Bremerton

Renton

Kent

Puyallup

Pullman

Longview

Richland

WA

Renton
30,000

Kent
23,000

CITY OF BREMERTON

OFFICE OF THE MAYOR ■ LOUIS MENTOR, MAYOR

Gateway to the Olympics and Home of the Puget Sound Naval Shipyard

Bremerton
36,668
Willow McGee
1990

Longview
30,000
city staff

Lynwood
26,930
city staff
1984

Richland
30,000
Dave Bryant
1989

Puyallup
21,290

Kirkland
36,620
city staff
1972

Pullman
23,270
city staff
1986

designer unknown
1989

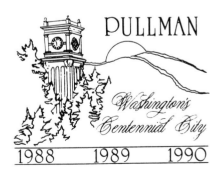

Everett
60,380
Steve Breeden, art director/designer
Chuck Howard, designer
Wayne Kilburn, designer
1990

The city of Everett's Office of Communications and Media Relations was established in 1990 by Mayor Pete Kinch. Handling all aspects of public relations for a city of nearly 70,000, they serve a very important function in the community. In order to be effective and proactive, government must keep the people it serves well informed.

The Office of Communications is a resource for all city departments offering graphic design, photography, special events and promotional assistance. The Office also works with local media, including print and electronic and produces a quarterly community newsletter. The department also administers the city's innovative City Hall at the Mall program, a unique satellite office designed to "bring government to the people."

City of Everett
Mastheads

Steve Breeden, art director
Chuck Howard, designer
Wayne Kilburn, designer

Steve Breeden, art director
Wayne Kilburn, designer

Wayne Kilburn, designer

Chuck Howard, designer

City of Everett
Communications/
Media Relations Dept.
Wayne Kilburn,
designer

Chuck Howard,
designer

Chuck Howard, designer
Henry Armijo, illustrator

Steve Breeden, art director
Chuck Howard, designer

Steve Breeden, art director
Wayne Kilburn, designer

Steve Breeden,
art director
Wayne Kilburn,
designer

Steve Breeden,
art director
Wayne Kilburn,
designer

WYOMING

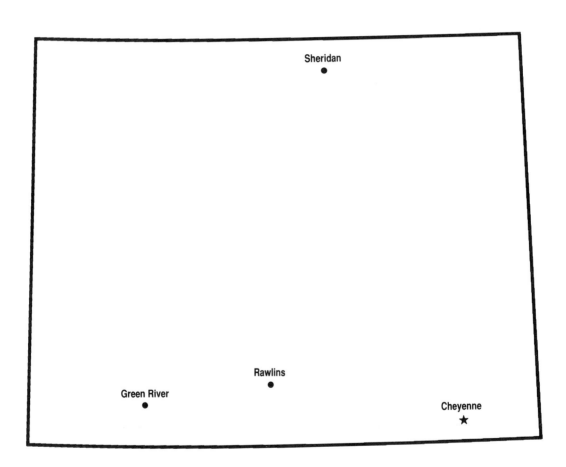

Cheyenne
50,000
city staff
1969

Rawlins
9,450
Paul J. Wawrziniack
1987

WY

Sheridan
15,146
1985

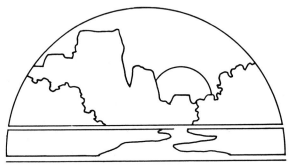

Green River
13,015
competition/Ilana Crow Thompson
1980

Mid
West

ILLINOIS

Highland Park
Des Plaines ●
Evanston
Downers Grove ●
Aurora ●
Bolingbrook

● Moline

Peoria
●

Champaign
●

★

Champaign
58,267
Chris Johns
1985

Bolingbrook
38,081
city staff
1978
city staff
1990

Moline
45,000
1985

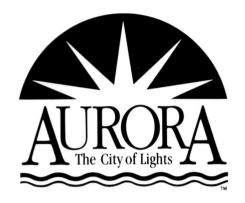

Aurora
85,350

Evanston
73,706
city staff

Highland Park
32,275
competition/Andre R. King
1987

Des Plaines
55,374
competition/Arthur R. Wetter
1960

Peoria
123,000
1975

Downer's Grove
45,000
city staff
1987

INDIANA

Fort Wayne

Muncie

Indianapolis

New Albany

Fort Wayne
180,000

IN

Muncie
77,217

New Albany
37,103

Government Cable

Indianapolis
792,000

Design Mark, Inc.
1983

IOWA

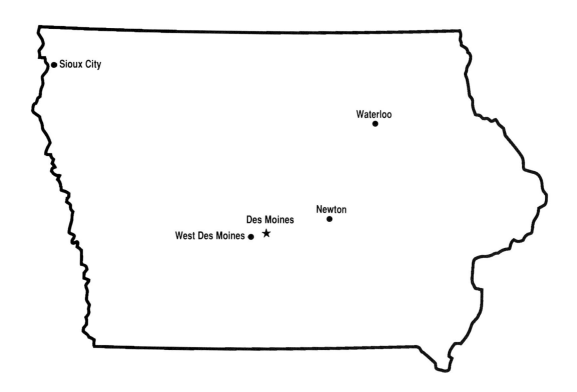

● Sioux City

Waterloo
●

Newton
Des Moines ●
West Des Moines ● ★

Newton
15,292
city staff
1988

Sioux City
83,000
Phillips Marketing
1984

Waterloo
75,000

Des Moines
191,004
city staff
1977

West Des Moines
30,000

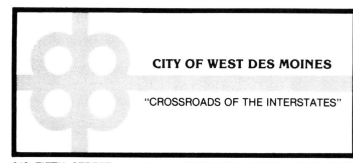

KANSAS

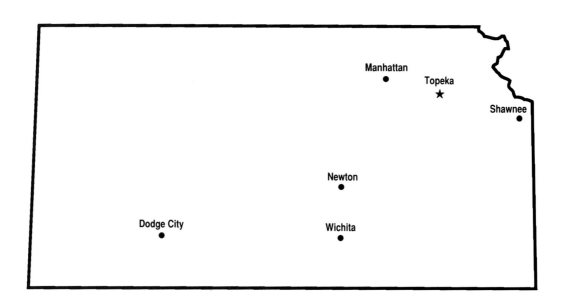

Topeka
141,280
Ed Bruske
1960

Wichita
300,000
competiton/William A. Boyle
1969

Shawnee
39,000
competition/Woody Ensor
1974

Newton
16,500
city staff
1970

Dodge City
21,000
High Plains Publishers
1983

Manhattan
33,750

MICHIGAN

Grand Rapids

★

Sterling Heights

Detroit

Dearborn

Ann Arbor

Grand Rapids
190,000
Joseph Kinnebrew
1980

Dearborn
91,000
1963

Sterling Heights
125,000

MI

Detroit
1,089,000
city staff
1958

Ann Arbor
107,800

MINNESOTA

Minneapolis
Plymouth ● ★
Bloomington ●

Winona ●

Plymouth
51,390
1973

Bloomington
87,000
Pegasus Corporation
1975

Minneapolis
356,840

minneapolis
city of lakes

Winona
25,400
Mediawerks
1987

Creating or acquiring a new logo for the city of Winona was not so much a deliberate process as it was a series of steps that more or less evolved into the adoption of what we now recognize as our city's identity.

Initially, the Winona Port Authority contracted a local advertising firm to have them prepare approximately 10,000 copies of an annual report and, as a part of that report, Mediawerks (the ad agency) included a stylized version of the heading "Winona, Minnesota". Sometime after the distribution of the report, the city staff asked the Port Authority Commission about the possibility of the City adopting their "Winona" heading as a new city logo. The Port Authority graciously agreed to the request.

Don Dennis,
Graphics Coordinator

MISSOURI

● Independence

● Kansas City

● Raytown

Overland ●
St. Louis ●

★

Springfield
●

● Joplin

Kansas City
1,299,700
city staff
1973

Springfield
160,000
city staff
1981

MO

Overland
19,620
1989

Joplin

Joplin
42,000
Wyrsch & Associates
1987

St. Louis
426,300

Raytown
33,000
city staff
1974

Independence
115,759

NEBRASKA

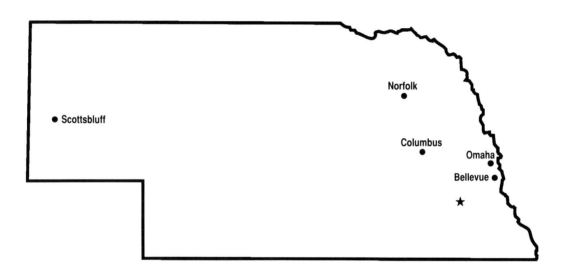

Norfolk

Scottsbluff

Columbus

Omaha

Bellevue

Norfolk
22,000
city staff
1982

Scottsbluff
14,156
city staff
1985

Bellevue
32,145

Columbus
18,360

Omaha
333.000
Jacob Hauck
1891

NORTH DAKOTA

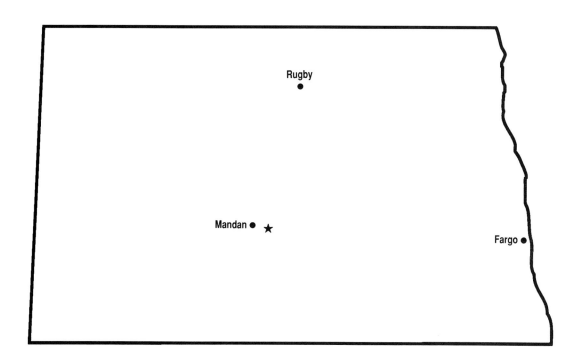

Rugby ●

Mandan ● ★

Fargo ●

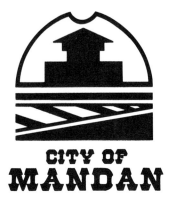

Mandan
16,057

Rugby
3,365
1940

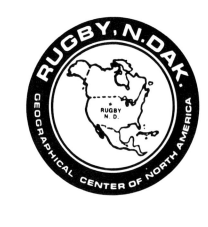

Fargo
74,000

OHIO

Cleveland

Columbus ★

Dayton
● Kettering

Hamilton
● Cincinnati

OH

Columbus
632,910
1982

Dayton
182,000
Penny/Ohlmann/Neiman
1990

Cleveland
535,830

Hamilton
65,000
competition/Jack Armstrong
1986

Kettering
62,000
city staff
1977

Cincinnati
500,000
Marcia Shortt
1980

Marcia Shortt
Laura S. Curran
Mary Beth Cluxton

CINCINNATI
POLICE

Cincinnati
additional logos

OKLAHOMA

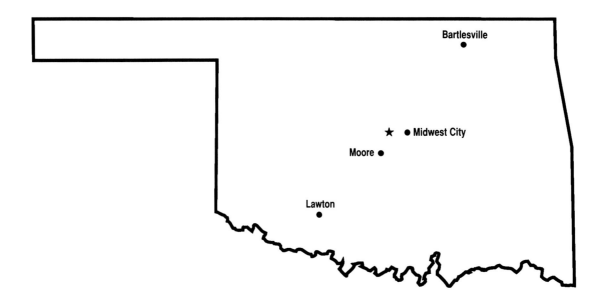

Bartlesville
35,000
1977

Midwest City
53,470
city staff
1968

OK

Moore
45,000
city staff
1983

Lawton
82,830

SOUTH DAKOTA

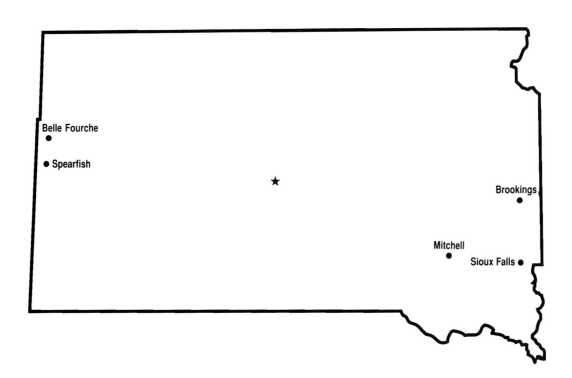

Belle Fourche

Spearfish

Brookings

Mitchell

Sioux Falls

Sioux Falls
100,000
city staff
1990

Spearfish
6,200
Wilbur Tretheway
1986

Belle Fourche
4,692
city staff
1988

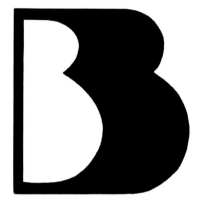

Brookings
16,280
1983

Mitchell
14,000

WISCONSIN

Green Bay ●

Manitowoc ●

Oshkosh ●

Sheboygan ●

● La Crosse

Madison
★

New Berlin ●

Racine ●

Kenosha ●

Oshkosh
53,534
Michael Paul Patterson
1983

New Berlin
36,000
Carol Brown
1972

Racine
81,588

 *City of Green Bay*

WISCONSIN

Green Bay
96,412
1958

Sheyboygan
48,484
DuFour & Associates
1987

Kenosha
77,752

Madison
175,830
Reed Design Associates, Inc.

La Crosse
50,000

Manitowoc
32,547
1989

South

ALABAMA

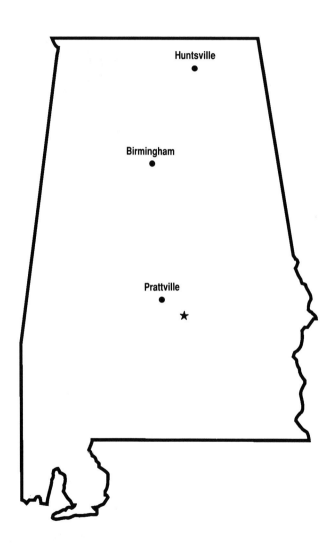

Huntsville
175,000
The Riley Co.
1989

A Future on the Horizon
Huntsville

Birmingham
277,510

Prattville
19,500
Maryanne Rogers
1991

ARKANSAS

● Rogers
● Springdale

Jonesboro ●

● North Little Rock
★ Little Rock

Rogers
25,000
city staff
1981

Two examples of national
awards bestowed to the city
of Rogers and others.

Springdale
30,000

North Little Rock
67,000
1984

Little Rock
181,030

Jonesboro
46,076
competition/Curtis Steel
1991

FLORIDA

Pensacola

Jacksonville

St. Petersburg

West Palm Beach

Jacksonville
609,860

Jacksonville
additional logos

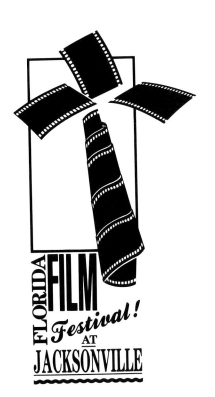

St. Petersburg
245,000
Ron Whitney
1983

Pensacola
65,000
city staff
1978

City of Pensacola

West Palm Beach
90,000
Laura Smith
1988

GEORGIA

Augusta •

Macon
•

Savannah •

Albany
•

GA

Albany
84,950

Macon
120,000
1925

GA

Augusta
47,532

Savannah
150,000
1987

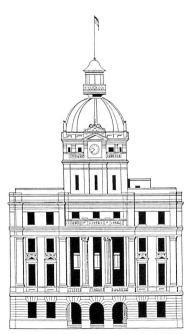

KENTUCKY

Paducah ●

★

● Ashland

Paducah
29,315

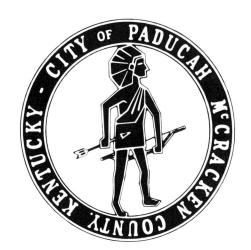

Ashland
27,000
David Carter Enterprises
1987

LOUISIANA

Houma

Baton Rouge

Lake Charles

Lafayette

Kenner

Alexandria

Alexandria
53,000
1976

Lake Charles
75,226
competition/David W. Dilts
1974

Baton Rouge
400,000

LA

Lafayette
90,000

Houma
96,568
1982

MISSISSIPPI

Pearl ● ★

Meridian ●

Biloxi ● Pascagoula ●

MS

MISSISSIPPI'S
FLAGSHIP
CITY

Pascagoula
29,318

Biloxi
50,000
Dr. Val Husley
1986

City of Biloxi

Established 1699

Meridian
45,000
1984

the City of
MERIDIAN

Pearl
23,000
1974

NORTH CAROLINA

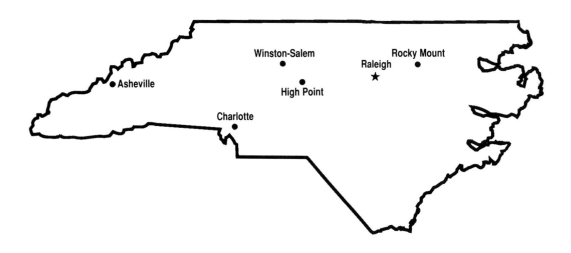

Winston-Salem

Rocky Mount

Raleigh

Asheville

High Point

Charlotte

Rocky Mount
52,000
Martha Daniel,
Daniel Design Associates
1984

High Point
75,000

Winston-Salem
150,000
Ginger Paterson
1988

designer unknown
1988

Charlotte
370,000
Design/Joe Sonderman
1980
Charlotte, NC

Q. **How did you get the assignment?**

A. *The firm was selected by the city through the City Manager and Director of Public Service and Information Offices.*

Q. **Were there special problems or challenges that you encountered in meeting the design objectives?**

A. *Because the city previously used the "crown" in various configurations, it was suggested that a renewed crown design would be appropriate. The crown image is historically significant in that the city was named after Queen Charlotte of England, and it was known as "the Queen City of the South." One other challenge that the firm overcame was inadvertant negative publicity given an earlier design study that became public knowledge.*

Q. **What kinds of design options were open to you?**

A. *Our options were somewhat limited due to the city's strong historical ties, though our firm concurred with the appropriateness of the crown as a symbol. The challenge to create a new crown, uniquely original, was great when considers all the probable crown designs, known and unknown to exist worldwide. Every method was applied to create a unique crown symbol that could be registered and copyrighted, while meeting the multiplicity of applications necessary for a growing municipality.*

Q. **How many roughs/comps did you present?**

A. *Though we developed many roughs, only two designs were presented to the city, and only one of those for the final presentation. The two designs were of the same theme but were significantly different in style.*

Q. **How did the client choose the approved design?**

A. *The final design was approved first through the City Manager's Office with final approval by the Charlotte City Council.*

Asheville
60,000
Doug Bean & Al Kopf
1988

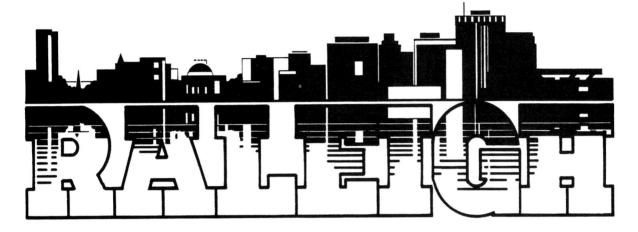

Raleigh
180,430
1985

SOUTH CAROLINA

Greenville

Rock Hill

Columbia
★

Sumter

Florence

COLUMBIA
A Capital Place To Be

Columbia
105,000

Greenville
58,370

Rock Hill
47,691
1985

FUNCTIONAL CITY

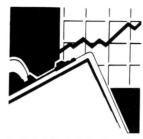

BUSINESS CITY

Rock Hill
additional logos

"The city logos: Business City,
Cultural City, Educational City,
Functional City, Garden City,
and Historic City are all theme
groups for Empowering The
Vision. Empowering The
Vision is a ten-year plan developed to help Rock Hill grow
and expand in these six theme
areas. The Rock Hill Economic
Development Corporation helps
to bring new businesses into
the Rock Hill area."

EDUCATIONAL CITY

GARDEN CITY

HISTORIC CITY

CULTURAL CITY

Florence
34,000
Mary Pat Fruetel

Ken Gasque Design & Advertising, Inc.
1990

Sumter
25,000

TENNESSEE

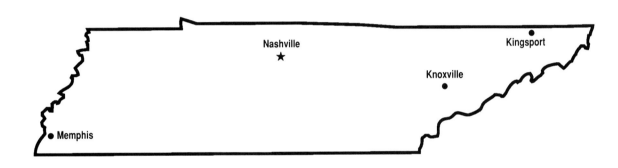

Nashville ★

Kingsport ●

Knoxville ●

● Memphis

TN

City of Memphis

Memphis
600,000

Knoxville
175,045
1990

Kingsport
32,027

Nashville
530,000
Herb Thompson, David Baker
    & Harold West
1963

VIRGINIA

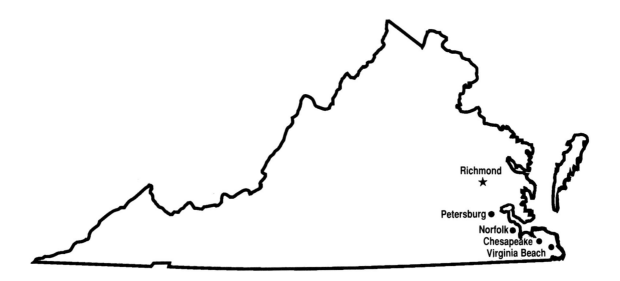

Richmond ★

Petersburg ●

Norfolk ●
Chesapeake ●
Virginia Beach

City of Norfolk

Norfolk
290,900

We Put Bright Ideas To Work

Virginia Beach
400,000
1963

"The first lighthouse erected by the United States after the establishment of the Constitution. Its construction was approved by President Washington on August 9, 1790. The Commonwealth of Virginia ceded two acres of land at Cape Henry to the new Federal Government and in 1791, a contract was signed by Alexander Hamilton and John McComb, Jr., bricklayer, for the erection of this lighthouse."

Richmond
203,056
Paul Nickerson
1975

Chesapeake
158,000
1963

Petersburg
41,000
city staff
1975

WEST VIRGINIA

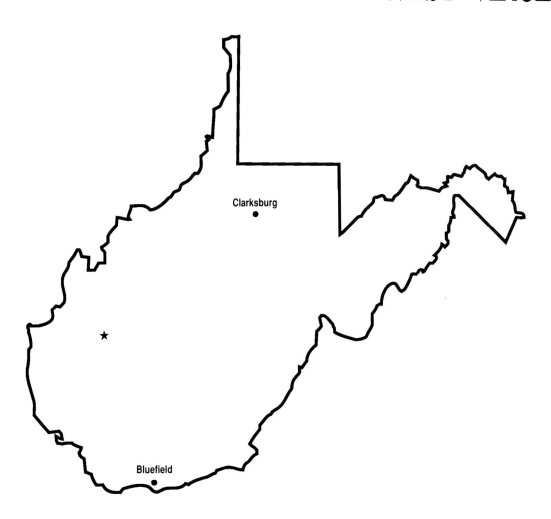

Clarksburg

Bluefield

Clarksburg
19,500

Bluefield
16,060
Rand Taylor
1939

CONNECTICUT

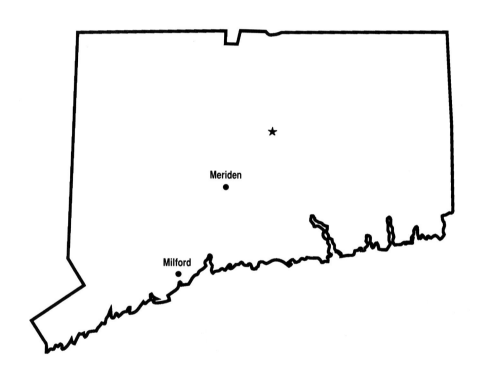

Meriden

Milford

Meriden
58,320
1868

Milford
52,400
city staff
1960

DELAWARE

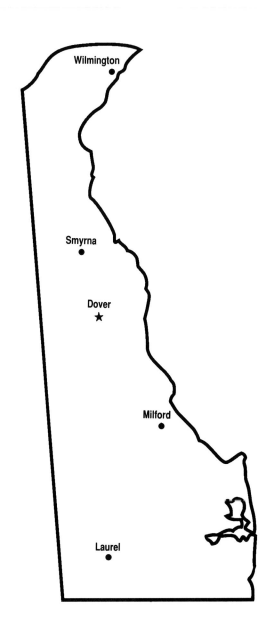

Wilmington

Smyrna

Dover ★

Milford

Laurel

Smyrna
5,500
C.D. Hodge
1984

Wilmington
69,690

DE

Dover
27,000

Milford
6,010
A. Calvin Ball
1937

Laurel
3.500

MAINE

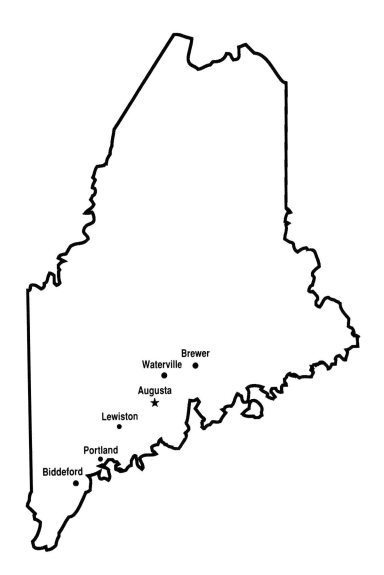

Brewer
Waterville ●
Augusta ●
★
Lewiston
●
Portland
●
Biddeford
●

ME

Augusta
21,819

Lewiston
40,481

Brewer
9,018
city staff
1986

Portland
63,000

Biddeford
20,200

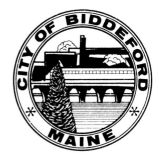

Waterville
17,000
Cynthia C. Michaud
1989

MARYLAND

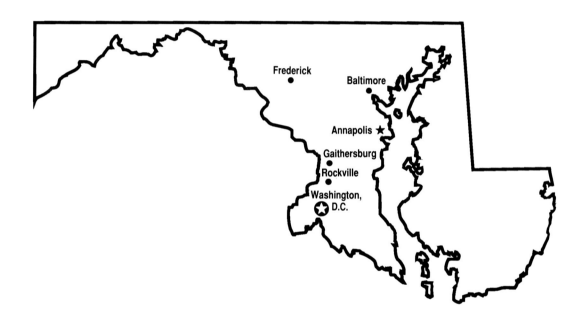

Frederick

Baltimore

Annapolis ★

Gaithersburg

Rockville

Washington,
D.C.

Erederick
40,000
Helen L. Smith
1979

Gaithersburg
36,000
1986

MD

Annapolis
37,500
Linda Lee Graphics
1983

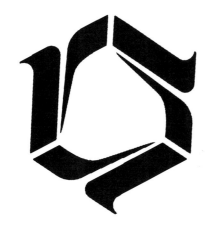

Rockville
45,600
Graham Associates, Inc.
1980

Baltimore
745,100

WASHINGTON, D.C.

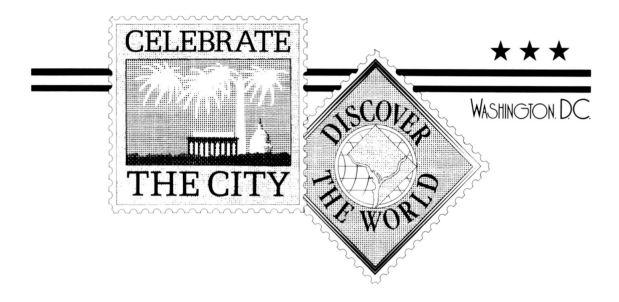

Washington, D.C.
626,000
city staff
1990

"The D.C. Committee to Promote Washington, is a quasi-government, non-profit corporation that directs Washington, D.C.'s national and inter-national advertising campaign and festivals program. This logo was created exclusively for the D.C. Committee to Promote Washington in 1990 for use in all advertising campaigns, special events and festival promotions, and on all promotional items distributed by the office."

MASSACHUSETTS

Boston ★

Newton ●

MA

Boston
573,600

Newton
82,011
city staff
1973

NEW HAMPSHIRE

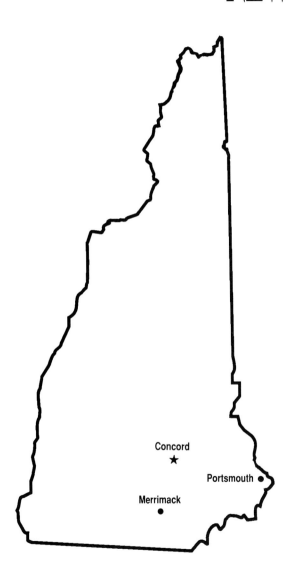

Concord
★

Portsmouth ●

Merrimack
●

NH

Merrimack
24,215

Concord
37,000
W.H. Piper

Portsmouth
26,254

NEW JERSEY

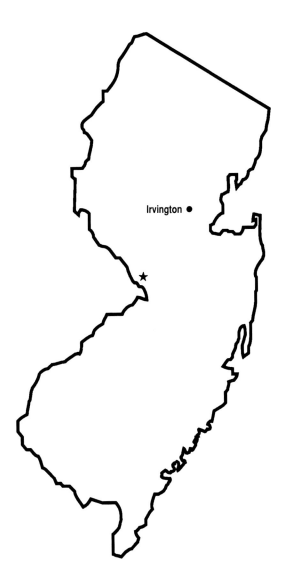

Irvington •

NJ

Irvington
61,493
city staff
1974

NEW YORK

Buffalo

Syracuse

Utica

Albany

New York City

Hempstead

NY

© 1986 City of Syracuse, NY

Syracuse
175,000
Robert Ripley
  Paul, John & Lee Agency
1986

Hempstead
738,517

Utica
70,000
Hank Godlewski
1983

DOWNTOWN UTICA DEVELOPMENT ASSOCIATION, INC.

New York
8,000,000
1966

City Graphics
1990

Albany
97,020

NY

GREATER BUFFALO CONVENTION AND VISITORS BUREAU

Buffalo
324,820

BUFFALO NAVAL & SERVICEMEN'S PARK

BUFFALO MUSEUM OF SCIENCE

BURCHFIELD ART CENTER

PENNSYLVANIA

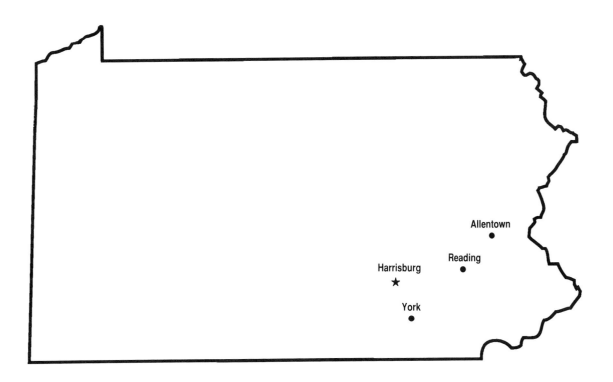

Allentown

Reading

Harrisburg
★

York

PA

York
44,900
J. Horace Rudy
1891

Reading
77,620

Harrisburg
51,530

Allentown
103,000
competition/Dick Wismer
   Media Resources
1990

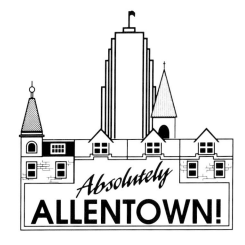

Chester
45,794
1866

RHODE ISLAND

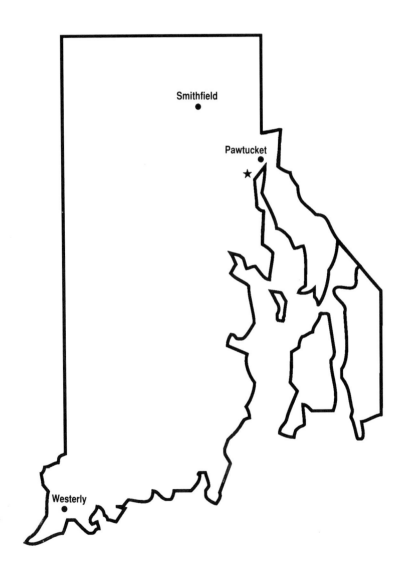

Smithfield

Pawtucket

Westerly

Westerly
19,000

Smithfield
16,886
city staff

Pawtucket
71,204

VERMONT

Montpelier

Barre

Barre
9,824
competition/Robert Young
1974

Montpelier
8,247
Tari Swenson
1991

Tim Newcombe
1990

Submissions

Submissions for the next publication of *City Symbols* is open to any new design or redesigned city, county, state, municipal entity or department logo not previously published in *City Symbols*. Noteworthy and trend setting designs will be featured with indepth interviews on how the design evolved.

Image Requirements:

1. Suitable line black & white stat (pmt) reproductions approximately 2"x 3" not to exceed 3"x 5" and a printed sample showing the ink colors.

2. If a screen tone is a part of the design, please supply camera ready pre-screened (133 line minimum) black & white print the same size as the line print. Extra fine detail on logo designs should be submitted on negative film.

Along with each submission please include the following information for typesetting purposes and mail to:
Design Publications, 13682 Rosalind Drive, Tustin, CA 92680.

Your name and title_____

City address_____

Population_____Date of logo design_____

Designer_____City Staff_____Competition_____Contract_____

There is no charge for logos submitted and selected for publication. A signed release must accompany each submission and logos will not be returned.

The city of _____grants Design Publications and its assigns the non-exclusive right to

publish and reproduce the official symbol of the city of _____
and related designs for the limited purpose of its inclusion in a work featuring approximately 400 city logos tentatively titled *City Symbols II*. The city waives any claim to proceeds arising from the sale of this work to cities, graphic designers and others.

I certify that I have the authority to act on behalf of the city when granting to Design Publications the non-exclusive right as described above.

By (print)_____Title_____   _____

Signature_____Date_____

Barbara Shaw is the principal of Shaw Design, a design and illustration studio located in Tustin, CA, specializing in corporate communications and logo design. Barbara has designed several logos for the city of Tustin and was the graphic/illustrator for the city of Brea. She has produced several books for Immigration and Refugee Planning, illustrated an inspirational self-help book and art directed/ designed two books of hair styles with co-author Marcia Divona.

Marcia Divona is a graphic designer and owner of Concept Design Studio in Tustin, CA. Her work has been exhibited at Orange County Center for Contemporary Art, Saddleback College, and Pacific Grove Art Center and she has won several awards. Marcia has collaborated with Barbara on numerous projects and books.

STOP